WHATEVER WILL THESE BECOME?

WRITTEN BY PETER GARLAND

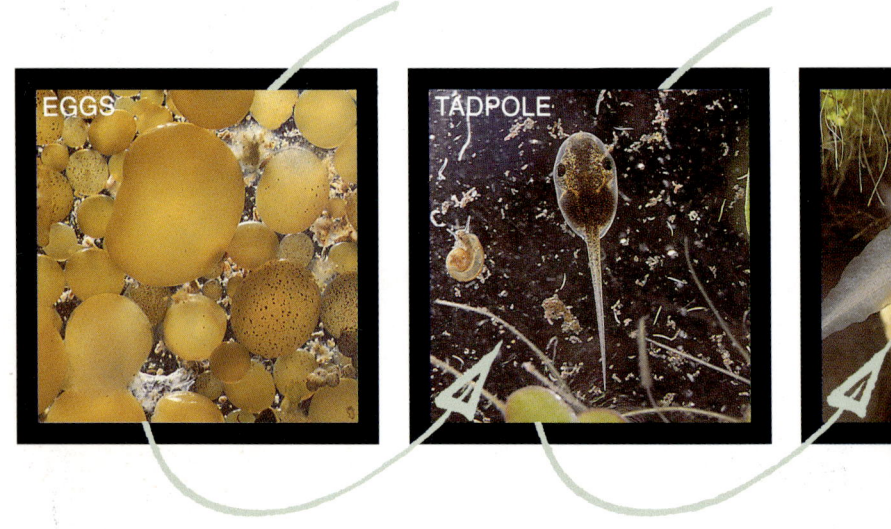

If a tadpole becomes
a frog,

FROG

and a piglet becomes
a pig,

and a wriggler becomes
a mosquito,

MOSQUITO

what will these be
when they're big?

If an acorn becomes
an oak,

and a blossom becomes
a plum,

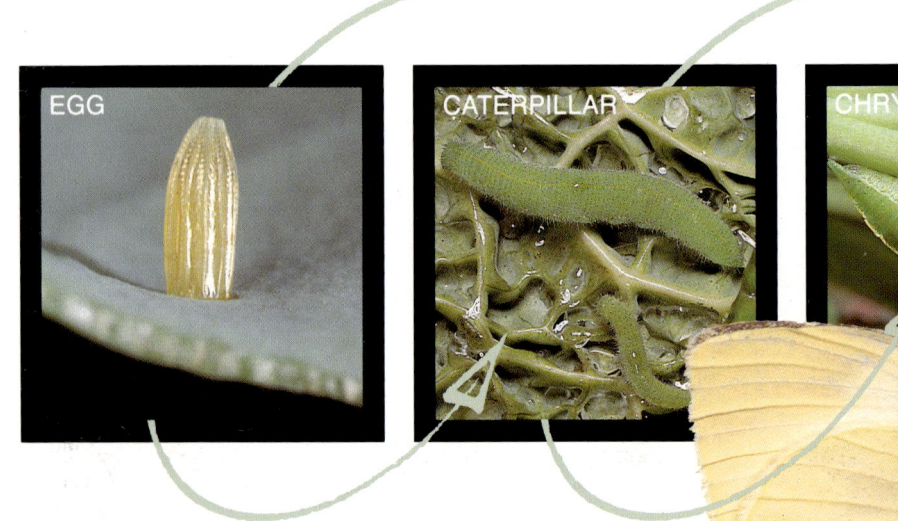

and a caterpillar becomes a butterfly,

BUTTERFLY

whatever will these become?